# GUESS WHAT'S COMING TO DINNER?

# GUESS WHAT'S COMING TO DINNER?

## THE EXTRATERRESTRIAL ETIQUETTE GUIDE

### SCOTT FIVELSON
### Illustrated by John Caldwell

BANTAM BOOKS
Toronto • New York • London • Sydney

GUESS WHAT'S COMING TO DINNER?
THE EXTRATERRESTRIAL ETIQUETTE GUIDE
*A Bantam Book / December 1983*

ISBN 0-553-34047-6

*Published simultaneously in the United States and Canada*

*Bantam Books are published by Bantam Books, Inc. Its trademark, consisting of the words "Bantam Books" and the portrayal of a rooster, is Registered in the United States Patent and Trademark Office and in other countries. Marca Registrada. Bantam Books, Inc., 666 Fifth Avenue, New York, New York 10103.*

PRINTED IN THE UNITED STATES OF AMERICA

CW 0 9 8 7 6 5 4 3 2 1

*FOR GORT*

# CONTENTS

"There are more things in heaven and earth, Horatio,
Than are dreamt of in your philosophy."
                    —WILLIAM SHAKESPEARE


"The idea of extraterrestrial life is an idea whose time
has come."
                    —PROFESSOR CARL SAGAN


"There's a sucker born every minute."
                    —P.T. BARNUM

# INTRODUCTION

In the past, discussion of the UFO phenomenon has mainly been confined to scholarly journals, like the *National Enquirer*. But gone are the days when a doorbell's chime could be safely assumed to announce nothing more startling than tiny creatures in brown beanies selling cookies. It is only a matter of time. You will open the door. You will see an extraterrestrial. Will you stick your foot in your mouth? Will he stick your foot in his?

To prevent that little faux pas that could lead to intergalactic warfare, this set of practical guidelines for both humans and extraterrestrials is essential.

Its purpose is two fold. First, it teaches Earthlings how to conduct themselves with decorum in any situation with an alien life-form. One small step for man, one giant step for manners.

Second, it addresses itself to outer space visitors who are also in desperate need of instruction in the proprieties. These instructions cannot be found in the writings of manners mavens like Emily Post and Amy Vanderbilt, who only *sound* like they're from outer space. This book proposes to teach the alien reader— if, indeed, he does read English—the proper etiquette when dealing with humans. If he does not read English, the book will teach him that binding tastes stringy.

As in any new social situation, you are likely to feel a bit awkward when meeting your first extraterrestrial. But if you maintain your poise, mind your manners, and refrain from pointing and screaming, "Them!" you're certain to be one popular Earthling.

Likewise, an alien who observes the social amenities is going to make more friends than one who goes around with a rude, to-heck-with-you, War-of-the-Worlds attitude. Of course, no alien can go from crater to grave without making an occasional blunder. All humans really ask of an alien is that he put his best three feet forward.

Today, humanity is at the brink of a great social frontier. If we are able to make friends with the teeming billions on distant planets, there's just no telling how much loot one might walk away with on a birthday. But if—as is equally possible—the extraterrestrials that you meet tend to be miserly or forgetful and if, time and again, they fail to live up to your highest expectations, please try to be understanding. Remember, they're only humanoid.

# CHAPTER 1

# PARTY ETIQUETTE:

## GUESS WHAT'S COMING TO DINNER?

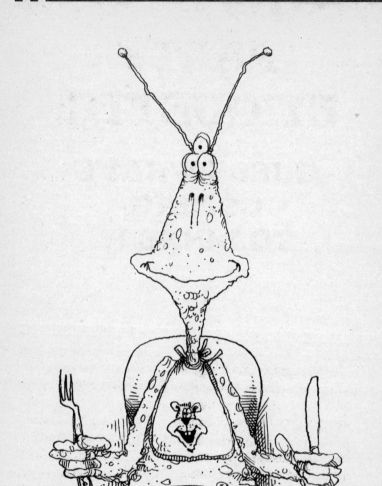

If the secret of entertaining an extraterrestrial is preparation, the second secret of the successful hostess if flexibility. Flexibility means not going into a tizzy because you're going to have to set an extra place for that Civil War soldier the alien abducted. It means serving *nouvelle cuisine*, and when the alien doesn't like it, going into the kitchen and coming out a minute later with a few isotopes on a garnished platter.

To be a good guest, the alien, too, should show some flexibility. He can start by leaving his planet to come here for dinner with plenty of time to spare, and not minding if he has to kill a little time on Earth until man starts walking erect.

# PARTY ETIQUETTE
# FOR HUMANS

## CREATING THE RIGHT
## AMBIENCE

As soon as you know that aliens are coming, there's always so much to do, especially since your help just resigned.

You will want to begin by protecting your home against radiation bombardment. This can be easily accomplished by lining the walls with rows of impenetrable material—the later works of Henry James, for example.

Once your house is secured, you can turn your attention to adding those little touches that will make the aliens think they've never seen a place so nice and homey.

Where to start? On the dining room table, set out a bowl of fresh fruit. And, just to play it safe, set out a bowl of plastic fruit, in case they like the taste of that better. (Make up your mind ahead of time not to get upset if you never see the bowls again.)

As you are tidying the house, you may find that the more you ponder the aliens' impending visit, the more ambivalent you feel about it. However, that's no excuse—it's still bad manners to keep lighted highway flares in your candelabras.

Although you should put all your energy into making

your home look its best, it is wise not to spend too much money preparing for the visit. When the aliens arrive, you will want to have a large nest egg in the bank, just in case they're coming to present you with the first four-billion-year utility bill for the sun.

## THE GUEST LIST

If the extraterrestrials are coming to Earth to look for intelligent life, you'll have to be picky in choosing which of your friends to put on the guest list. Since it is quite likely you won't come up with enough to round out the table, you should try to think of any acquaintances who might add some sparkle to the evening in other ways. For instance, if you know a person with a history of hallucinations or mental instability, inviting that person to come to your soirée without telling him it's going to be an extraterrestrial dinner party might be fun!

## WELCOMING AN EXTRATERRESTRIAL

It is bad manners to go completely rigid and stutter, "Th-th-this is n-n-n-not r-r-r-r-really ha-ha-ha-p-p-p-pening."

Don't make his welcome a solemn occasion. Show him you're glad to meet him. Step right up to the alien, say, "Give me 15!" and slap his hand. (Note: When greeting an extraterrestrial in France, kiss both cheeks on *each* of his heads.)

# PET ETIQUETTE

No matter how grotesque your alien guest turns out to be, howling, whimpering, or hiding under the sofa is always unbecoming. And your dog shouldn't do it either.

# ACCEPTING GIFTS

No alien likes to show up on a planet empty-handed. Thus, you can probably expect to receive some token offering at the door.

If the alien brings you a box of candy or flowers, express your gratitude. On the other hand, if the gift the alien brings you is the secret of nuclear fission, don't take the wind out of his sails by telling him we already have it. Simply be gracious and say thank you.

Besides, maybe you can rewrap it and give it to some underdeveloped country.

# PARLEZ-VOUS FRANÇAIS?
# SPRECHEN SIE DEUTSCH?
# SAY WHAT?

Unless your alien guest was found frozen in the Arctic, conversation is usually the best way to break the ice. "How do you like those Dodgers?"—said while good-naturedly slapping what passes for the extraterrestrial's shoulder—will go a long way toward showing him just how advanced our civilization is. But suppose the alien you meet speaks his own special brand of gibberish. For the considerate Earth host, there is always a way.

If an extraterrestrial does not speak English, play charades.

If an extraterrestrial does speak English, you may still run into problems. Remember, even if he's capable of solving four-dimensional Rubik's cubes, he will probably not possess a native speaker's grasp of English. Hence, in order to avoid misunderstanding, you must look at language anew, always taking care to say the right thing.

# LANGUAGE DO'S

1. If an alien has one or more clones, it's perfectly all right to say, "He's good people."

2. If an alien has three or more arms, it's also all right to say, in the course of a discussion, "On the one hand . . . But on the other hand . . . Now on the *other* hand . . ."

# LANGUAGE DON'TS

1. It is always bad form to tell an alien, "Why don't you stop drinking? You're loaded to the gills." Unless, of course, he has gills.

2. If an alien is trying to become a freelance writer, do not encourage him to "send out a feeler."

3. When introducing an extraterrestrial, do not say, "Meet my ex-," unless you were once married.

4. Don't tell an alien he's looking blue.

5. No matter what you say to an alien, don't promise him the moon.

# BODY LANGUAGE

Because the English-speaking alien may have difficulty putting all his feelings into words, it behooves the host to watch for and interpret physical cues. Certain of these cues should be easy enough to interpret. For instance, a giant pincer cracking your skull like a walnut means "No."

# TIMING YOUR DINNER

It is always difficult to predict when aliens are going to arrive, especially if they're looking for your house (and your planet) for the first time. Still, a hostess usually likes to work with some kind of rough plan. Therefore:

- Light the coals one half-hour before your guests are expected.

- When a blip appears on the radar screen, throw the steaks on the grill.

- When wind-up monkeys start clapping their cymbals, the refrigerator opens and food flies out, screws turn slowly in the front-door hinges, and a blinding light blazes through the smoking keyhole, *dinner is served!*

# SEATING ARRANGEMENTS

Always reserve the seat at the head of the table for the person whose civilization is oldest. Persons whose civilizations have destroyed themselves and are just starting over can bring up a bar stool and squeeze in somewhere.

Etiquette does not forbid inviting two extraterrestrials,

one of whom is the other's natural predator, but it's your responsibility to take whatever precautions are necessary in order to prevent any scenes.

So, don't seat them next to each other. And, for God's sake, serve enough food!

## WHAT TO SERVE

You don't have to serve prime rib in order to please your alien guests. In fact, they don't even mind having leftovers. Just remember, never reheat pork with a phaser.

---

### HINTS FOR THE HOSTESS

1. Never try a new recipe when you are having an alien over for dinner, especially if he has no mouth.

2. If you can barely see an E.T.'s heartlight because it's caked over with cholesterol, use margarine instead of butter.

3. On the other hand, if the alien whom you are entertaining possesses the ability to change shape at will, you probably don't have to worry about trying to keep the meal low-cal. In fact, the only thing that you should be concerned about is the chance that your guest, when served his food, might look at Gramps, lick his lips, and say, "I don't want a sandwich. I want a Manwich." If this should occur, etiquette dictates that someone immediately rise to help Grandpa onto the bun.

---

# CHOOSING A WINE

When choosing a wine to serve at dinner, the punctilious host never departs from these four basic rules:

- Red wine with a red creature.
- White wine with a white creature.
- Club soda with a creature who is transparent.
- Champagne with a creature who is a gaseous mass.

# DINNER CONVERSATION

Though your alien guest might wind up carrying the conversational orb, it is more than likely that you, the host, will be doing most of the talking as you respond to your guest's questions about the Earth and its history. (Of course, this will not be necessary if the alien's society already has this knowledge, especially if they've been filming our history and watching it back on their planet, accompanied by a laugh track.)

You may not be an expert, but you can still field most of his queries. For instance, if he wants to know about evolution, tell him about Charles Darwin. Then, if he wants to know about fossils, tell him about President Reagan.

# "OH, BLOURP, YOU'RE SUCH A CARD!"

Dinner is over. You've all had a few, and no one is feeling any pain. It's at a time like this that an alien, if he has any personality at all, cuts loose, and the fun *really* begins. Regenerating bald spots with his index finger; stopping and starting his heart as a gag; on Halloween, bobbing for Apple computers—an alien can be the lifeform of the party!

Although the playing of after-dinner games may be the high point of your evening, you, the host, should never lose sight of the welfare of your guests. A responsible host *does not* allow an intoxicated alien to dance the limbo under a laser beam.

However, even if the alien is loaded, don't offer to drive his saucer home. (Face facts: It's safer to let an inebriated alien drive than a sober Earthling who has never been behind the wheel.)

# THE PARTY'S OVER

You've tried drumming your fingers on the table. You've tried yawning and saying, "Well, it's been a big day." But, though this being understands English, he just doesn't seem to get the message. What is a hostess to do?

When you find yourself saddled with an extraterrestrial who doesn't know when to leave, the rules of good conduct suggest that you get up from your chair, stretch, and subtly maneuver your guest toward the door while exposing him to any of the following:

- *Extreme heat*
- *Extreme cold*
- *Electricity*
- *Fire*

If none of these methods causes the alien to say, "Well, I've really got to run," then you are left with no other recourse. It is time to call in a nuclear strike—or pull out the sofa bed.

# PARTY ETIQUETTE FOR EXTRA- TERRESTRIALS

*Because this is, after all, a total extraterrestrial etiquette guide, it would be a breach of etiquette to leave out tips for our guests from outer space. Therefore, this section has been included for the edification of any alien wishing to conduct himself with charm and good taste during his visit to Earth.*

## DON'T FILL UP, ALIENS!

*Since your hostess will be slaving all day to create an Earth dinner just for you, it's important to show up with a healthy appetite. So have a light lunch: hydrogen or helium.*

## WHEN SHOULD AN ALIEN SMOKE?

*It is permissible for an alien to smoke right after he has crash-landed, at least until the fire truck arrives.*

# FIRST IMPRESSIONS COUNT

*At least they do to NASA. So oblige your host by letting him make a few plaster casts of your footprints.*

*If dinner isn't ready by the time your footprints have dried, just relax and make small talk, like explaining the origin of the universe.*

*If it's a big bash with many of the host's friends and relatives in attendance, an alien should get up and mingle before dinner, though not with anyone's atomic structure.*

# THE IMPORTANCE OF POSTURE

*There is only one thing worse than an extraterrestrial who slouches. That's an extraterrestrial who stands up straight and knocks a hole in the ceiling. If you're that kind of extraterrestrial, be considerate. Slouch.*

# TABLE MANNERS FOR ALIENS

*An alien with breeding and refinement is one who never fails to observe the following rules when he sits down to eat:*

1. *Never telepath with your mouth full.*

2. *If you're going to eat the silverware, always work from the outside in, starting with the implement that is farthest from the plate. (Only a boor heads straight for the dessert fork.)*

3. Never use X-ray vision to find out what kind of filling is in the pie. (However, heat vision may be used if the pie arrives cold.)

4. If you are an alien plant, do not play rootsy under the table.

5. Chicken should not be eaten with the fingers. Fingers should be eaten separately.

6. Your host is serving brisket, but your sensors tell you "NO." If you want to avoid offending this well-intentioned Earth host, politely push your food around on your plate. If you can't stand to touch it, use telekinesis.

7. If you should happen to belch, immediately cover your mouth with your hand and say, "Excuse me. Swamp gas."

8. It is perfectly acceptable to use a light saber for cutting steaks and chops. It is the height of gaucherie, however, to eat peas off a light saber.

# CHAPTER 2

# HOUSEGUEST ETIQUETTE:

## ANY PLACE I HANG MY HEAT SHIELD IS HOME

**W**hether he's coming to Earth for a weekend or for a more extended invasion, an alien always prefers being a houseguest to having to check into some motel. Unfortunately, many hosts are intimidated by the prospect of opening their door to an alien creature. They needn't be. Having an alien around the house is just like having another child. The only real difference is that what a kid tracks in doesn't burn a hole in your linoleum.

But whatever the drawbacks, they're more than compensated for by the appreciation that an alien will show to a host who provides him with his creature comforts.

There's just nothing worse than being alone, three million light years from home, and sleeping on a lumpy mattress.

# HOUSEGUEST ETIQUETTE FOR HUMANS

## THE GUEST ROOM

Before an alien arrives to take up residence in the guest room, a host should always inspect the accommodations with the following checklist in hand:

- Does the bed have a nearby wall outlet in case your guest wants some "juice" in the morning?

- Have you left reading matter on the nightstand— classified government documents, maps of military installations, and so on? And, in case he wants gossip from back home, is there a copy of *Clay People* magazine?

- Is there a sewing kit in the bureau for the alien? A soldering iron for his droid?

- Is there an overnight light-saber recharger in the guest bathroom?

## WHEN A HOUSEGUEST BRINGS A GIFT

When an extraterrestrial presents you with the gift of immortality, a thank-you note is in order. And don't take forever to write one!

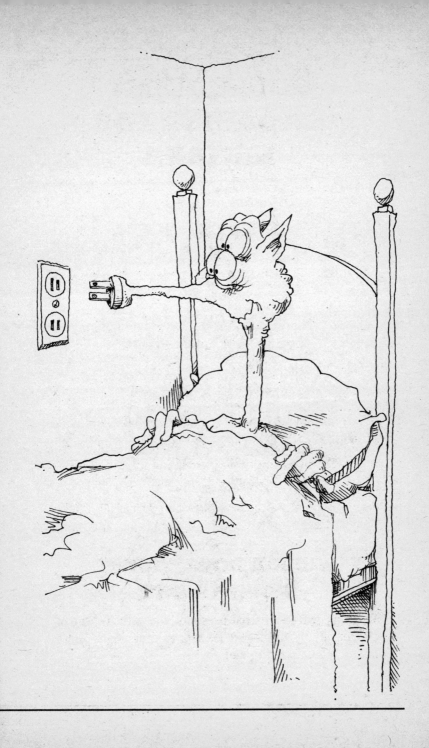

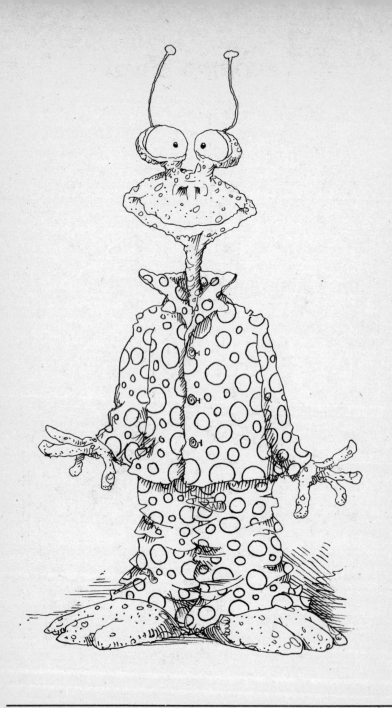

# PHONING HOME

During the time that an extraterrestrial is staying as your houseguest, there is a good chance that he is going to be monopolizing your umbrella. Aliens are absolutely compulsive about talking on the umbrella, and this is liable to cause you some inconvenience, especially when it's raining. To avoid knock-down, drag-out fights over who gets the umbrella, let the extraterrestrial phone home as much as he wants. Buy him a Totes.

# UNMARRIED COUPLES

"Should two extraterrestrial plants be allowed to stay in the same vase without the benefit of matrimony?"

It's the kind of tough-to-answer question that can cause any host a sleepless night. Since it's not a matter of etiquette, but really one of conscience, no absolute statement of what is right or wrong will be ventured here. All that will be said is that if the hostess does see fit to let them spend the night together, she does not have to cater to their request to be put in a vase filled with vodka.

# PAJAMA PARTIES

If you've never had a pillow thrown at you with 50,000 pounds of thrust, you've never had aliens over for an extraterrestrial pajama party.

Here is the kind of sleepover that teenage girls really enjoy. And the key to a successful pajama party—besides lots of munchies—is asking the extraterrestrials to bring along some of their favorite records.

To please everyone, put a stack on the hi-fi—some of yours and some of theirs. That way you can listen to a disc containing all of the knowledge of their elders, immediately followed by "Jam Up, Jelly Tight" and "Hanky Panky"!

# WHEN AN ALIEN GETS THE SNIFFLES

It's always better to put off that fishing trip than to let an extraterrestrial come for the weekend with a virus that could wipe out the planet.

Obviously, if he is here already and comes down with something, you don't want to fool around. You tell that extraterrestrial to march back to bed this instant. Then, with the help of the Air Force, isolate your house in a plastic bag. Administer treatment along these guidelines: Starve a cold, feed an Andromeda strain. Of course, the considerate host always postpones a visit by Martians if he himself is coming down with a common cold.

# HOW TO TAKE AN ALIEN OFF YOUR FACE

No matter how relaxed your alien guest begins to feel, there is still such a thing as an alien getting a little too familiar. You can avoid unnecessarily hurting his exoskeleton and his feelings with the following polite but effective measures for saving face:

1. Grope your way to the kitchen, relying on your senses of hearing and touch.

2. Bend over the sink, and run the alien under hot water for 30 seconds.

3. Tap the perimeter of the creature gently but firmly with the handle of a butter knife.

4. Twist the alien counterclockwise. Voila! The alien twists off easily. (Once you have removed the alien, immediately check the underside to see if you've won a trip to a distant planet!)

If, with this method, you do not achieve the desired results, the extraterrestrial has forfeited all right to civil treatment. It's time to get tough. Though you may not have the stomach for it, the following is suggested:

1. Grope your way to the den.

2. Flick on the power for your stereo system.

3. Position your head between two speakers.

4. Put on "Ebony and Ivory."

5. Watch the alien fly out the window.

# BEING REPLACED

Particularly if a visitor from outer space is here on business, there is a strong probability that he will want to take over your body. If you had other plans for your body and it's too late to change them, tell him so. If not, it is incumbent upon you to cooperate and be a good host. Before you become a mindless slave, it is always nice to inform your friends and relatives by mailing out a formal announcement, which might read as follows:

> MR. ED JOHNSON
>
> HAS THE HONOR OF ANNOUNCING
>
> THAT HE WILL BE REPLACED
>
> BY AN EXTRATERRESTRIAL LOOKALIKE
>
> ON SATURDAY, THE FIFTH OF JUNE,
>
> AT TWO O'CLOCK

Once the announcement is mailed, you can rest assured that in future weeks you will not have to say to friends: "No . . . there . . . is . . . nothing . . . wrong. . . . Why . . . do . . . you . . . ask?"

# HOUSEGUEST ETIQUETTE FOR EXTRATERRESTRIALS

*Although every alien who comes to Earth should behave courteously, this is never more true than when an extraterrestrial stays as a houseguest. It's a time for thoughtfulness, for consideration, and, if the host is short on beds, for alien plants to grab a pillow and offer to sleep in the vegetable bin.*

## TRAVEL LIGHT, TRAVEL RIGHT

*How much should you pack when staying with Earthlings for the weekend? Keep it to a minimum. First of all, though outer space is infinite, closet space may not be. Besides, suitcases have a way of seeming to get heavier as you go, especially when you are coming to Earth from a weightless environment.*

*Whatever you do decide to bring, make certain you pack all important accessories. Before you close your luggage and zip up your garment bag, ask yourself, "Have I got my jetpack? My astro-belt? How about that clingy shirt with the sunburst on it?"*

## CURB YOUR TAUNTAUN

*The nicest thing that you can possibly do for your Earth hostess is not to show up with an alien pet in tow. Your hostess is going to have enough to do the week of your visit without the added job of going around cleaning up Tauntaun poop.*

*And don't forget, a guest always compensates his hostess for a vacuum cleaner that breaks because the fan housing got clogged with Wookiee hair.*

## JUST BE YOURSELF

*Nobody is going to want to spend time with an extraterrestrial who is always "on"—always destroying things. If you are honest with yourself, you will realize that when you are destroying everything in sight, you're doing it because you think it's expected of you. Just be yourself. And start destroying the things you sincerely want to destroy.*

*The people of Earth will respect you for it.*

## DON'T BE AN E.T. WITH B.O.

*It's all right if an alien's ship leaves a vapor trail. Not so for the alien. Having been through a meteor shower is not enough. E.T. need bath!*

# 10 DO'S AND DON'TS FOR THE EXTRATERRESTRIAL HOUSEGUEST

1. *Don't track mud on the ceiling.*

2. *Don't leave antimatter in the driveway.*

3. *Do strip the bed when leaving, but don't throw the dirty sheets in the hamper. (Your hostess may want to have them analyzed.)*

4. *Do return anything you borrow: sports equipment, gloves, safety pins, your host's identity.*

5. *Don't put your feet on the coffee table, especially if you're not sitting on the sofa.*

6. *Do offer to help with household chores, unless you're all thumbs. If you are, let someone with five different types of fingers try to do it.*

7. *Never use an atom smasher to cut a frozen bagel.*

8. *Remember after you shower: Saturn has rings, bathtubs do not.*

9. *Don't leave scales in the drain.*

10. *If you want to be asked back, don't disintegrate your host and hostess.*

# CHAPTER 3

# RESTAURANT ETIQUETTE:

## EARTH—THE FINAL SMORGASBORD

**B**efore an extraterrestrial takes off on his ship and goes back to the grind, it would be a pity if he didn't allow you to take him out to a few Earth restaurants. Suggest pub crawling in London, or crawling anywhere else he might like. There is no question that his astronomical research is a matter of consequence, but at 5 p.m., it's time to get down to some *gastronomical* research.

In addition to remembering the rules of restaurant etiquette, your extraterrestrial guest should make a point of paying your tab at least once during his visit. Short of dissection, it's the best way to show you that his heart's in the right place.

# RESTAURANT ETIQUETTE FOR HUMANS

## WHERE TO DINE

When you're taking an extraterrestrial out to sample some Earth cuisine, the possibilities are so diverse, it's hard to pick just one. Should you take him to that lively little Mexican place? Should you hit the best steakhouse in town? Whatever you choose, remember, if an intergalactic council is going to decide the fate of our planet based on the quality of this meal, avoid any restaurant where there's never a wait.

Of course, just as important as the meal itself are the surroundings in which it is eaten, and the more they resemble the alien's native planet, the better. Therefore, if he's accustomed to an atmosphere with noxious gases, take him to Gary, Indiana. Or, if the alien is accustomed to no atmosphere at all, take him to Pizza Hut.

## MAKING SUBSTITUTIONS

If the alien doesn't see anything on the menu that he'd like to order, take the initiative and find out from the waiter if it would be possible to make a substitution. Instead of the onion rings, could your friend have a basket of breaded nuclei? Don't they make any other kinds of hero sandwiches—like John Glenn on a kaiser roll?

# RESTAURANT ETIQUETTE FOR EXTRATERRESTRIALS

*When an Earthling goes to the trouble of taking an alien out on the town, the least his outer space visitor can do is observe the rules of restaurant etiquette. The polite alien is one who makes an effort to avoid those acts which make waiters scream in horror, such as carelessly crashing through walls or pouring ketchup on a Chateaubriand.*

## RESTAURANT PARKING

*Always tip the attendant who parks your saucer unless, when he brings it around, you notice a new dent.*

## THE CHECKROOM

*An E.T. always checks his umbrella, unless he's expecting a call. (Note: A female alien does not check her fur if her fur does not come off.)*

## SUMMONING A WAITER

What are you supposed to do when you want the Parmesan cheese, but your waiter only comes by about as often as Halley's comet? In Europe it would be perfectly acceptable to whistle or clap your hands, but in America an alien needs to employ a subtler approach.

And so, without attracting attention, glance around the room until you finally sight your waiter. Then, turn on the tractor beam.

## WHEN AN EARTHLING MAKES A MESS

Any Earthling who thinks an alien is the most ghastly sight imaginable has obviously never looked in a mirror while he was eating barbecued ribs. In fact, when you dine for the very first time with a human who is having ribs, you will constantly be looking for a way to make him more palatable to the eye without causing embarrassment.

The most effective and tactful step to take is to freeze time. While the hands of clocks, patrons, waiters, and busboys remain transfixed, simply dunk the tip of your napkin in your untouched water glass and spend two or three minutes mopping the hot sauce off the Earthling's face and hands.

When the job is done, and time is unfrozen, the Earthling will be at it again, so you'll probably want to repeat this procedure at intervals throughout the rib dinner. Though it may be a slight inconvenience to you, it will improve your enjoyment of the meal. And when the Earthling's done, he'll be so proud of himself. He won't even need a towelette!

# PICKING UP THE CHECK

*If an E.T. says, "I insist," and picks up the check, it is unseemly, when he sees the tab, for him to say, "OOOOUUUCCH."*

# "JACQUES, THE MEAL WAS INCOMPARABLE"

*Restaurateurs always appreciate a compliment from a happy patron. That's why, when an alien really enjoys a meal, he should give a restaurant four stars—if he owns that much land back home.*

# CHAPTER 4

# BUSINESS ETIQUETTE:

## MISSILE WHILE YOU WORK

**W**hether it's because he wants to put down roots or stand on his own six feet, the extraterrestrial who has any intention of staying on Earth sooner or later decides it's time to stop mooching off humans and get a job. For a traveler from beyond the stars, it's the start of an incredible odyssey. IN baskets. OUT baskets. Frightening creatures like time-systems analysts. And, if he thought Darth Vader was an S.O.B., wait till he meets his boss.

Only by knowing the unwritten rules that govern the workplace on Earth will an alien be able to succeed in business. Maybe it's enough where *he* comes from, but on Earth you need more than gravitational pull.

# BUSINESS ETIQUETTE FOR HUMANS

## HELPING AN ALIEN FIND A JOB

The moment that an alien announces that he is tired of being a no-account space bum and that he is going to get an Earth job, the first thing you must do is take him into the den for a serious talk. You must remind him that no matter how strange the world he's from might be, he is about to set foot in a world that is far more bizarre—the business world.

Since personal appearance is so important in the business community, your initial instinct might be to tell him, "Ya know, I think you'd be great at a phone job." But you should also consider the possibility that the alien's appearance can act as a plus. Ask around. Maybe there's an office that's looking for someone to come in once a week and cure hiccups.

Whatever the alien decides is his strongest selling point, you should advise him of the wisdom of lining up interviews without delay. The time for him to look for a position is now, when the field is wide open—not when the other 10,000 ships from his planet start to arrive.

# AN EMPLOYER'S OBLIGATIONS

Once you have hired John Q. Alien, it is up to you, his employer, to see that he has everything he will need to function efficiently in the workplace. Does he have a rubber claw to wear when sorting Xerox copies? Does he have a filing cabinet for when he runs out of space in his pouch? Work aids such as these help make for a happy extraterrestrial instead of one who always has one eyestalk on the clock.

## A GOOD BOSS IS ADAPTABLE

It's quite a shock for the alien who has come to conquer Earth to discover that if he is going to do it, he'll have to start in the mailroom. That's why a boss—though he can't have employees laying eggs on company time—should be willing to bend the rules a little, make a few concessions, in order to ease the alien's transformation into a working stiff.

One area in which the boss can practice the fine art of compromise is the alien's coffee break. If the alien explains that it is his custom to work, then take a coffee break, in alternating thousand-year cycles, give your okay, as long as he agrees to do the thousand-year work cycle first.

# HANDLING AN ALIEN CLIENT

Handling alien clients isn't any harder than handling human ones, most of whom are accustomed to making inhuman demands anyway. Still, some words of advice are warranted if you hope to conduct yourself properly when the man in the gray flannel pseudopod comes to see the new ad campaigns.

To start, do not allow your meeting to be constantly interrupted by telephone calls. If the phone rings as an alien comes off the elevator and walks in your door, discreetly say to the caller, "I'm sorry, Bill. Some *thing* just came up. Can I call you later?"

If the meeting is going to include a sales presentation, let the length of your talk be determined by your alien client's response. A sure sign that an alien client is beginning to get bored is if he's starting to crack his knuckles. An even surer sign is if he's starting to crack yours.

Although it's sometimes tough to know just what your client wants (astro-zombies tend to be the worst in this respect), you'll keep the account as long as you maintain a good working relationship. The secret here is to remember that often business is transacted better in casual surroundings. So don't turn him down if he asks you to spend a few days at his winter home in the Bermuda Triangle.

# LADIES FIRST!

She may be an extraterrestrial, but remember—she's also a woman. So the next time you happen to enter the office together, don't forget: A female alien *always* oozes under a door first.

# BUSINESS ETIQUETTE FOR EXTRA-TERRESTRIALS

*Since, as far as we know, no extraterrestrial is an island, every alien who relocates to Earth can benefit from a knowledge of business etiquette. In fact, nothing is more essential to an alien's transition from spaceman to businessman, except for enlarging his wardrobe with a few new suits that don't have screw-on helmets.*

## TIPS FOR THE EXTRATERRESTRIAL ON A JOB INTERVIEW

1. *Never present a glowing letter of recommendation.*

2. *In the box on your job application marked "Previous Experience," do not list previous lives.*

3. *Do not ask if employees get a day off on Ming's Birthday.*

4. Don't tap your foot, twiddle your thumbs, or emit beeps.

5. A recommendation from "a group mind" counts as one *reference*.

6. When talking about why you want the job, don't criticize the planet you came from. The interviewer will only figure that next you'll be criticizing Earth.

7. Say "No," if you're asked if you smoke, drink, or go to the proton races.

8. Explain to the interviewer why you would be an asset to his organization. Show him that there are other reasons to hire you besides to help fill their quota of Martian-Americans.

# WHEN AN ALIEN WORKS FOR AN ALIEN

*Except for being an alien's valet (or, as they call it in England, an extraterrestrial's extraterrestrial), no other job is quite as rewarding as being an alien's personal secretary. The reason it's so fulfilling is that the responsibilities are so many. You are expected to type, file, keep accounts, and collate, usually all at once. You are relied on to screen all incoming telepathic communications, putting through only the most important and putting all the rest on hold. Sometimes you're even required to accompany the boss on trips to other planets, although*

*you* do not *have to agree to stay in a cabin with an adjoining airlock.*

*Your own good appearance will reflect well on your boss, who will also be looking for an alien who can transform itself into a human. If you can only remain human for a few hours, don't despair. You can still apply for work as a "temp."*

## GET DOWN TO BUSINESS

*To an alien who is new to the working world this may sound cold and callous, but do not bring your personal problems to work with you in the morning.*

*So you just heard the psychic cries of a billion kinsfolk as your planet exploded. We've all got our little problems. Now, Glimnok, where's that report?*

## PERSONAL CALLS

On the job, the rule concerning personal calls is simple: Don't phone home.
E.T. phone home, E.T. get canned.

## BE WILLING TO STAY LATE

UFOs are capable of impressive aerial acrobatics. However, it does not impress a boss when an alien makes an abrupt 180-degree turn and shoots off at a tremendous speed when he's asked to stay overtime.

## THE OFFICE ROMANCE

When an alien "gets involved" with an Earthling at the office, it doesn't matter if they use discretion: Gossip travels at Warp Factor 1. The wise alien is the one who steadfastly avoids the storage-room tryst. Do your work at the office, and your docking in space.

# GOOD WORK HABITS FOR
# THE ALIEN

1. Never leave empty pods in your desk.

2. Always hide the interspace communicator you are trying to build before you leave at night.

3. Do not use your expense account to finance the repair of your ship.

4. Do not magnetize other people's paper clips.

5. Do not stab coworkers in the back. Just insert a small electronic device in the back of the neck.

6. Do not sit around with the door closed, firing at a photo of the boss with a ray-gun.

MEADOWLANE
COUNTRY CLUB
ANNUAL
ROAST

# PUBLIC SPEAKING

*An alien businessman who develops a standing in the community will undoubtedly be asked from time to time to address various civic groups. As this is good public relations for both his firm and his planet, the successful life-form should accept invitations to speak whenever possible.*

*In preparing his speech, an alien should keep in mind that no address, no matter who delivers it, can be a total success without a strong opening. "People of Earth, you are doomed" is usually a good attention-grabber.*

# QUITTING

*When leaving a job, you should always give your boss two weeks notice in order to give the company time to try to find a replicant.*

# GETTING FIRED

*Even if you are blameless, a human employer can have you bounced if he catches your droid taking indecent liberties with a telex.*

*Remember, in the job world, your reputation stays with you. So, if your employer regretfully informs you that you are being let go, don't melt anything. Otherwise, future references will say things like, "Does not cope well with failure . . . tends to melt things. . . ."*

# FOR THE SELF-EMPLOYED ALIEN

*In today's busy world, it is not considered discourteous for the self-employed alien to use a phone-answering machine.*

*What is nice about an answering machine is it's so easy to use. All an alien has to do is leave a short recorded message, stating his whereabouts and promising to be in touch with the caller as soon as possible. For instance, if he's home but can't come to the phone at the moment, his message might sound like this:*

Hi, this is Zybor. I'm in suspended animation right now, but if you'll leave your name and number, I'll get back to you in the 21st century.

*Callers should not start speaking until after the droid beeps.*

# GOOD JOBS IF YOU'RE WILLING TO TRAVEL

*Given the current economic state of the planet Earth, an extraterrestrial must face the fact that he might not find a job. But if he doesn't, it's not so bad. Earth isn't the only planet. As a matter of fact, there are many exciting, new areas in outer space, with plenty of room for an ambitious, young alien.*

*After all, the universe is expanding!*

# CHAPTER 5

# SPORTS ETIQUETTE:

## GRACE UNDER ATMOSPHERIC PRESSURE

The scene is easy to picture: A group of human beings is shooting hoops on a neighborhood court when a group of extraterrestrials comes along and suggests a little pick-up game. The players are quickly divided into two teams—"Shirts" and "Scales"—and what promises to be an exhilarating athletic event is about to begin. However, no sooner does play commence than a violent competitiveness arises, and playing the game for the fun of it is swiftly replaced by playing to win. A tentacle trips a foot. An elbow breaks an antenna. Tempers flare. And the next thing you know, an Earthling is being slam-dunked into another dimension.

It is to forestall precisely this kind of unfortunate, but all too likely, scenario that humans and aliens both must learn to observe the principles of sportsmanship, as well as the special regulations that apply to Earth games when involving alien participants. Hopefully, droids, too, will make an effort to play by these rules, although if they don't, one can't get too angry, because, as they say, droids will be droids.

# SPORTS ETIQUETTE FOR HUMANS

## PITCH WITH POLITENESS

It is extremely discourteous for an Earthling who's pitching to roll the baseball across the plate and claim that it fell within E.T.'s strike zone.

## WHEN ACCIDENTS HAPPEN ON THE RACQUETBALL COURT

The considerate Earthling always stops and helps the alien up, offers an apology ("Sorry about that"), and grants him time-out to grow a new arm.

## WHY THERE ARE NO GOLF COURSES ON VULCAN

A golf course is a place where an extraterrestrial who tells you that he has no emotions finds out just how wrong he is. (Note for Earth linguists: It is also a good place to hear words in the alien's language that you've never heard before.)

If your usually rational golfing partner is screaming

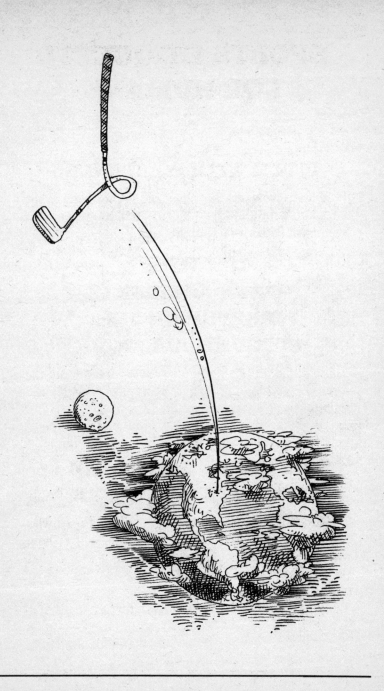

Vulcan obscenities after dubbing shots which he knows he had no logical reason to dub, the rest of your foursome would be well advised to stay out of club-throwing range until this Vulcan's amok time is over.

If this behavior persists throughout the morning, have pity on the pointy-eared duffer. Get a couple of beers into him before you play the back nine. Then remind him, high score wins!

## TO KEEP PLAY ON THE GOLF COURSE MOVING

Always take them up on their offer when a foursome of transparent aliens tells you to "play through."

## BOXING AMENITIES

Because the last thing an extraterrestrial needs is cauliflower earflaps, an Earthling should always go easy when sparring for fun with an outer space being. Sure, you want to mix it up a little, see if he's light on his suction cups, but neither of you will have a very good time if your pal has to spend the whole afternoon with his nose tilted back beneath a mound of green-stained Kleenex.

So instead of going for the KO, content yourself with boxing for points. If the alien starts to get rough, *then* you can give him a fat mandible.

## WATCH OUT FOR HUSTLERS

Beware of the extraterrestrial who makes a big show of not knowing how to hold a cue yet is willing to play for money. His last residence prior to Earth was probably a mining colony, where he did nothing for months but shovel zirconium ore and shoot billiards.

Of course, he won't take you to the cleaners at first. He'll start out by letting you win a few games. But watch out when this alien, who was chalking the wrong end of his cue just a minute ago, walks up to break, calls out pockets on four different tables, and "puts a little Martian on the ball"!

## TALLYHO!

Nothing makes the blood race or the heartlight blink like a pack of yapping hounds given the scent of a Speak & Spell game, and then let loose to lead a mounted field of scarlet-coated huntsmen galloping over hill and dale in hot pursuit of an E.T.

If you want to put some spring in his step and ensure a merry chase, members of the hunt may wish to sport on their belts huge rings of jangling keys.

As for the E.T., he will go to any length to elude capture. However, it's a violation of the rules for E.T. to emit a protective mist, except when he finds himself in open country and needs to use the lavatory.

# SPORTS ETIQUETTE FOR EXTRA-TERRESTRIALS

*Whether an extraterrestrial can ever go pro and model his own line of sportswear isn't nearly as important as whether he is able to display that quality known as sportsmanship. Nobody likes an alien who loses fair and square and then blames his loss on sunspot activity. That's because graciousness in defeat is perhaps the true meaning of sportsmanship, except in those special instances where the alien is extremely large, in which case sportsmanship means taking over any shot he wants.*

## WHEN AN ALIEN IS ODD MAN OUT

*When, in picking sides for baseball, an alien is the last one left to be chosen, he should not roll into a ball and sulk—unless the teams need a ball.*

# BE GRACIOUS ON THE GRIDIRON

When it is "4th and 10" and no one knows if the quarterback will pass or punt, it is highly unsporting for an extraterrestrial defensive lineman to do a mind-probe.

# RULES ARE FOR ALIENS, TOO

Just because you're the fastest thing ever seen on a basketball court doesn't mean you won't get spotted when you try to commit an infraction. You say you have eyes in the back of your head? Well, spaceman, refs do too. And they'll be all over you in an instant, more than happy to give out free throws.

So remember:

- Time traveling with the ball is illegal.

- Levitating an opponent is a personal foul.

- And make it your motto, you alien hot-doggers, no three-hand set shots!

# "LAST ONE IN IS A ROMULAN EGG!"

*Swimming can be enjoyed by extraterrestrials young and old as long as you mind your manners around the water and follow these simple guidelines:*

- *Call up your local park district and find out what hours have been set aside when extraterrestrials can use the pool. If the park has made no such provisions, show up at the pool in human form. (This will create fewer problems than if you change in the bathhouse before and after you swim.)*

- *If you are a slime creature from outer space, please bring your own towel.*

- *High dives from the Mother Ship into the pool are prohibited.*

- *You and your extraterrestrial buddies may be able to hold your breath for two weeks,* but the lifeguard doesn't know that. *Give him a break. Don't horse around.*

# CHAPTER 6

# DATING ETIQUETTE:

## TENDRIL IS THE NIGHT

With a bright red ship custom-built for extra speed, and lines like "How's about a soda in a parallel universe?" an alien might be able to land a date with *some* girls, but not the kind he'd want to bring home to meet his Overlords. Dating a *nice* girl requires an entirely different approach, even if she knows in her heart it's a case of love at first sighting. Thus, both human and alien are required by propriety to play the game of Earth courtship, and it's been that way since the first ancient astronaut went gaga over an Inca.

# DATING ETIQUETTE FOR HUMANS

## DON'T KEEP AN EXTRA-TERRESTRIAL WAITING

When an alien shows up for a date, keeping him waiting doesn't increase the mood of romantic anticipation. It only gives him more time to consider vaporizing your parents. If you harbor the least bit of affection for that couple who gave you life, powder your nose and get downstairs.

## BE CONSIDERATE OF YOUR PARENTS

The time when a young woman starts to date an alien is always a very trying period for her parents. Parents worry when a daughter goes out with someone from an older civilization. They know he is apt to do things that someone from a civilization as young as ours might not be ready for.

Hence, to put your parents completely at ease, your alien date should always state what time he expects to bring you home, adding an hour to allow for collecting plant samples, buzzing sheep, and so on.

Once you've left the house, you and your date can show your thoughtfulness by remembering to inform your parents if your flight plans change. Mom and Dad don't want to be mean. They just want to know where you are. All you have to do is call and say, "The gang is going to Pluto after the dance. Can I go, too?" Most times, if you just ask your parents, they can be pretty cool.

## AN IDEAL DOUBLE-DATE

If you and your friend both happen to fall for the same extraterrestrial, don't compete. Let one of you get to know him. Maybe he has a clone!

## WHEN A YOUNG LADY NEEDS A CHAPERONE

If you and your extraterrestrial date want to park inside a black hole, not only *may* the Force be with you, young lady, the Force *must* be with you.

## BREAKING UP WITH AN
## EXTRATERRESTRIAL

Show the alien you respect him enough to know that he can handle it. Sit him down the next time you're together and tell him it's over. Don't worry. It won't be the end of the world—unless he gets *really mad*.

## DON'T BE A CHEAP PICK-UP

There is nothing worse than a girl who's got a reputation as a cheap pick-up. We all know the type. The kind who hangs out at the corner, waiting for an alien ship to fly by, ready to jump at any old line as long as a grappling hook is attached.

Sure, any girl would like to take a ride in a UFO. But if you care about your rep at all, wait for the ship to land!

## WHEN ESCORTING A
## FEMALE ALIEN

Remember, at the end of the evening, when bringing an alien back to her ship, always walk your date to the airlock.

Simple as it sounds, it holds the potential for some embarrassment, especially if an Earthman is unable to find the airlock. Of course, it's not your fault that the alien's saucer is seamless. But making her wait for you to find the door and open it for her can very easily blow the mood you've worked all night to create. If after 15 minutes you're still stumped, give her a peck on the cheek and be on your way.

The next day, be sure to send flowers.

# QUESTIONS MOST COMMONLY ASKED BY TEENAGERS

Q: Is it permissible for a female alien to ask an Earthman out?

A: The *female* alien should always wait to be asked by the *male* human. But there is nothing wrong with her planting a little subliminal suggestion—"Devils Tower, Wyoming . . . Say, sevenish?"

Q: My extraterrestrial steady is so possessive, he's driving me crazy. At first, I didn't mind spending all of our time together, but now apparently that's not enough. He wants to ingest me into his protoplasm. He tried once already last night. What should I do if this happens again?

A: Explain from a few feet away that you're feeling trapped by the relationship and that you're not going to allow him to turn you into a boring blob. If you have to walk out the door, it may be painful,

but take my word for it, staying would only be more painful.

Q: What do I do if my alien boyfriend wants to go "all the way"?

A: Understand that you are talking about a *very* close encounter. Even if you consider yourself an experienced young woman, you may not be prepared for such an encounter. Remember, an extraterrestrial's index finger may not be the only appendage he has with a tip that glows.

Q: I am an average American guy. Is it old-fashioned of me to want to marry an extraterrestrial virgin?

A: No, not at all. Many men want to boldly go where no man has gone before. As for wanting to marry an extraterrestrial—well, it takes all kinds.

# DATING ETIQUETTE FOR EXTRA-TERRESTRIALS

*Even if an extraterrestrial is Big Man on campus, he won't necessarily be a dating success. If an alien's the shy type, the kind who likes to spend his time looking like inanimate objects, the odds are girls will act as if they don't even know he's alive. In order to attract more than compass needles and metal shavings, the alien must learn to be aggressive. No woman wants to be the invader!*

## MAKING A DATE

*Too many aliens think they can ask a girl out at the last minute. As much as a girl would like to go to the prom with an extraterrestrial, she is not about to sit at home, waiting for the phone to melt.*

*That's why an alien should always call for a date several weeks in advance. And when he makes the date, it should be for a Friday or Saturday, not for a schoolnight. Parents frown on schoolnight dates unless it's a special occasion, for example, if the alien got tickets to a sporting event or he's going to a TV station to tape an ultimatum for the people of Earth.*

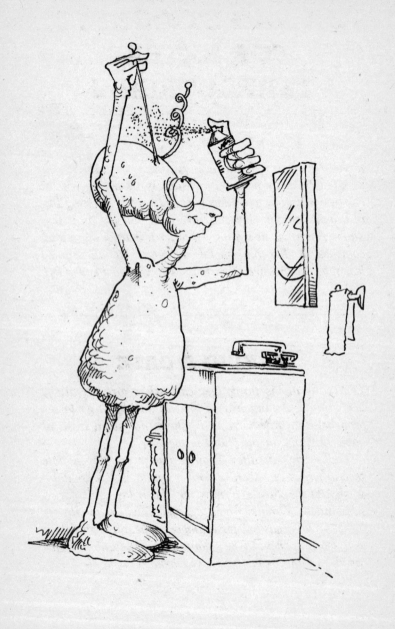

## BE A HANDSOME CREATURE

*Girls love a man in uniform, so if you have one, wear it, though you may want to pay a tailor to take the thunderbolts off the sleeves.*

*Since you want to look your best, a haircut is also in order. And here's a grooming tip: If two antennae are all you have atop a bald, green head, take a cue from balding Earthmen, who have devised a brilliant way to make the most of what they've got. Disguise that pate. Get a perm.*

## BRING YOUR DATE HOME AT THE APPOINTED TIME

*Even though his ship can travel faster than the speed of light, the polite alien does not bring his date home before they left. Not only would it worry her parents, but it would put his date in the position that evening of needing another date.*

*If you are consistently bringing your date home an hour before you left, make a point of correcting this habit. Next time, try to bring her home only a half hour before you left; the time after that, arrive when you left (Be careful! Don't bump into each other!); and so on, until finally, you're walking your date to the door a minute before curfew.*

## AN ALIEN CAN TURN ON THE CHARM

*Without a doubt, a male extraterrestrial has certain advantages over his Earth counterparts when it comes to romance. For instance, while an Earthman on the make must physically turn the lights down low, all an extraterrestrial has to do is suavely cause a power failure.*

## BREAKING A DATE

*An extraterrestrial breaks a date only if the lack of some vital element in the Earth's atmosphere is killing him, and even then, with sincerest apologies.*

# CHAPTER 7

# WEDDING ETIQUETTE:

## SOMETHING BORROWED, SOMEONE BLUE

$\textbf{N}$ext to the coming-out party that the armed forces may throw for a crash-landed alien when it crawls out of the crater, its wedding will be the most important event in its extra-terrestrial life. The wedding can be as large and elaborate or as small and simple as the alien itself. But whatever you choose, when an extraterrestrial is involved, you want to make it extra-special.

This chapter will offer advice to humans and aliens together, because it deals with that most blessed of occasions, the joining in holy matrimony of a human and an extraterrestrial in an intergalactic mixed marriage.

# THE WEDDING ANNOUNCEMENT

When an extraterrestrial and a human finally decide to tie the knot, the wedding is announced by the mother of the Earthling, traditionally with a bloodcurdling scream.

In addition to this announcement, you will also want to send invitations. The rules applying to these invitations are the same as with any wedding, except that when you send invitations to alien relatives who will not receive them for 500 years—even if mailed at the speed of light—reply cards may be omitted.

If the site of the wedding is far removed, enclose a map with all invitations. If the wedding will be nearby, just leave a trail of Reese's pieces.


# PLANNING THE WEDDING

There is always a lot to attend to when an extraterrestrial marries a human, like going for a blood test so the human can find out if her intended has any, and registering for gifts at Lockheed. Everyone is so harried in the months before the wedding that you should be glad to accept the help of the alien's family: there is simply more to do than is humanly possible.

First on the agenda, you must decide on clothes for the bridal party. You can't go wrong if you opt for the formal look of top hats and tails, particularly because the extraterrestrial's side may only have to buy headgear.

Next on your checklist will be the hiring of a caterer

for the reception. Depending on the nature of the extraterrestrial's family, you may not want a caterer who charges by the head.

And perhaps most important is the employment of a photographer to record the event. At the end of the party, when the aliens give every member of your family a posthypnotic suggestion wiping out all memory of the experience, your last coherent thought—as your eyelids flutter and close—can be how glad you are you didn't leave the picture-taking to Uncle Fred.

## THE WEDDING CEREMONY

The procession does not begin until the Mother Ship has landed. Once the engines are quiet, the organist starts the wedding processional—the five-tone melody from *Close Encounters.*

The bride and groom will be married by the clergyman of their choice, who should end the service by saying a few words on a pertinent theme, like "We Are Not Alone."

When the service is over, the bride and groom walk down the aisle as the organist plays the triumphant wedding recessional—"The Theme from Star Wars."

## THE RECEIVING LINE

When attending the marriage of an extraterrestrial and a human, it is not polite to walk through the receiving line with a geiger counter.

# THE RECEPTION

The success of the wedding party will largely depend on just how well you attended to a variety of details. Did you remember to place LARGE centerpieces in front of the most gruesome aliens? The festive spirit you've strived so hard to create can be lost in an instant, simply by making a small faux pas like seating a clone at the droid table.

But if you've done your job well, you can breathe a sigh of relief and enjoy the party like any other guest. Plunge a Ritz cracker into a chopped liver landing pod. If you're an alien, why aren't you on the dance floor? Join tentacles and dance the hora!

# THE HONEYMOON

With a string of antigravity boots dangling in its wake, the bride and groom's ship will whisk them off on their honeymoon. The only question is, which moon? Don't ask. Newlyweds like their privacy.

# CANCELING THE WEDDING

Though sad to contemplate, there is such a thing as the broken engagement. To save your guests the time and money they may be spending in preparing for the wedding, they should be informed as quickly as possible.

The breaking of an engagement between an extraterrestrial and a human is traditionally announced by the sounding of the "All Clear" on an air-raid siren.

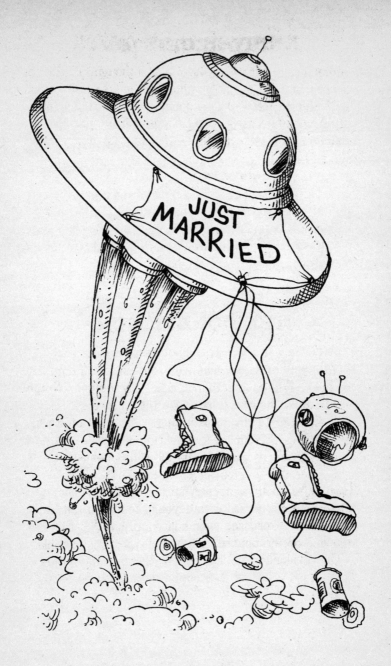

# ANNIVERSARY GIFTS

Although any gift will be viewed as a thoughtful gesture, a present with symbolic value will undoubtedly mean something special to the couple. With a little ingenuity and, in some cases, security clearance, you can remember *their day* with these classic anniversary gifts:

| Anniversary | Gift |
| --- | --- |
| First | Hydrogen |
| Second | Helium |
| Third | Oxygen |
| Fourth | Nitrogen |
| Fifth | Carbon |
| Tenth | Titanium |
| Twenty-fifth | Uranium |
| Fiftieth | Plutonium |

In the first few years of marriage, especially if money is tight, the couple themselves may only exchange cards on their anniversary. By the time these extra-terrestrial-and-human mixed marriages exist on Earth, greeting card companies should offer a wide array to choose from. It should be noted at this point that it is not advisable to give an extraterrestrial an insulting card unless you have a *very* strong marriage. Safer and nicer by far is a card with depth of feeling, a card that sensitively expresses what's in your heart. A card like the one on the opposite page.

*For a Very Special Life-form*
*On Our Anniversary*

*I know you always understand,*
*my darling swirling mass,*
*it's hard to know what words to use*
*when talking to a gas.*
*But still I'd like to say*
*what you know telepathically:*
*I love you, dear, for what you are.*
*Whatever that may be.*

**Happy Anniversary**

# CHAPTER 8

# ABDUCTION ETIQUETTE:

## MARS WITHOUT CASH

The proper amenities have now been set forth for both humans and extraterrestrials in all the key social encounters traditionally dealt with in an etiquette book. However, no *extraterrestrial* etiquette book could possibly be complete without a discussion of the alien's favorite kind of get-together—the abduction.

An abduction by aliens is a chance to open your mind and forget all you have ever known about space, time, the universe—but *not* what you know about manners. If anything, you should be even more eager to pleasantly interact, because if you don't get along, it is hard, in deep space, to walk out in a huff.

As it happens, there are some situations that occur during the course of an abduction for which an Earthling is not prepared by the general rules of decorum. That's why a UFO should never hit a human with a paralyzer ray unless he looks like the kind of well-bred person who knows his abduction etiquette.

# ABDUCTION ETIQUETTE FOR HUMANS

## ABDUCTEES DON'T CHEW GUM

If you are chewing gum, dispose of it before you board the saucer. *Do not* surreptitiously stick it to the bottom of the saucer. If everybody did that, the saucer would never get off the ground.

## OVERCOMING SHYNESS

It's easy when you're being abducted to get such a bad case of nerves that you lose the power of speech. But did you ever stop and think about how this looks to your alien hosts?

That's right. Not exactly Mr. Sociable.

But you *can* become outgoing in the company of your abductors if you just look your fears in the eye and say, "What am I afraid of?"

Because, when you really think about it, what's the very most they could want from you? A few locks of hair? Fingernail clippings? One of each of your organs?

# GUEST ACCOMMODATIONS ON A UFO

When you're traveling in Europe, you don't expect the same standards you find at home. Likewise, when you are abducted by aliens, you should be prepared for less than Class A accommodations.

But even if your quarters aren't fancy, at the very least, you can expect them to be clean. That means there is *a fresh force field* over the seat of the commode when you're shown to your cabin.

If there isn't, ring the bridge!

Incidentally, unless you want the craft you're on to explode like the Death Star, *do not* plug in your blowdryer without an intergalactic current converter.

And, finally, a little reminder: It is the height of rudeness to change channels when Ming is on the viewscreen. (It is also punishable by death.)

# POISE IN A WEIGHTLESS ENVIRONMENT

Anyone can learn to be poised and confident in a weightless environment—to suavely push off from a wall and somersault over to a shapely humanoid while sucking a cocktail out of a Glad bag. All it takes is practice. Of course, the best kind of practice is walking around in a weightless environment with a book on top of your head. Not only does keeping a book on top of your head help you develop poise, it cushions the blow every time your head hits the ceiling.

## WHEN TO RISE

In a weightless environment, a gentleman rises whether a woman enters the room or not.

## HOW TO COPE WITH A PHYSICAL EXAMINATION

You have been stripped and placed on a table, and the aliens are about to examine your body. Remember, they probably won't know much about the parts of you they'll be touching.

Sit back. Enjoy.

## HOW TO COPE WITH A BRAIN DRAIN

If, when draining knowledge from human brains, they finish with you faster than with everyone else, try not to take it personally. (However, when you get back to Earth, it might not hurt to renew your subscription to *Newsweek*.)

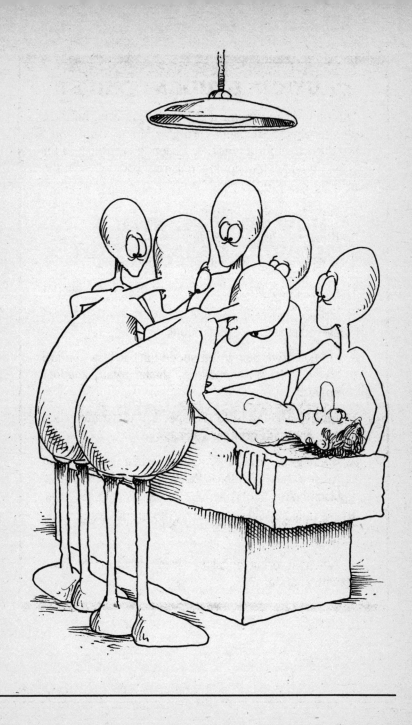

# CAUTION: STUDENT DRIVER

After you have traveled the first quadrillion miles or so, your alien host might turn to you and ask if you'd take the wheel for a while. In order to be prepared for such an event, you should familiarize yourself with the following rules of the road:

1. Never tailgate an asteroid.

2. Klingons *always* have right of way.

3. A flashing yellow light means supernova.

4. Always stop and look both ways before coming out of a time warp.

5. Never pass on a spiral nebula.

6. Do not drive below the speed limit unless you are trying to trick Klingons into thinking you have lost power.

7. Always accelerate to the speed of the traffic when merging with orbiting vehicles.

8. Backing is prohibited, except when you've failed to see the WRONG WAY sign and entered a black hole.

9. Never make the jump into hyperspace if you don't have a muffler.

10. When entering a galaxy-sized life-form, proceed with caution.

# AN ABDUCTEE NEEDS
# A HOBBY

The flight back to your abductors' planet is probably going to take years, so bring along a book by James Clavell. (Suggested reading: *Tai-Pan*, if you're staying within our galaxy; *Shogun*, if you're traveling beyond it.)

# THE TROUBLE WITH TRIBBLES

It's easy for an Earth abductee to start putting on a few pounds, just sitting around on a spacecraft during a journey across the stars. If you begin to notice that there's not as much room in your cabin as there used to be, it's time to lay off the chocolate-covered Tribbles.
    Tricorders don't lie.

# WHEN AN ABDUCTEE IS
# RETURNED TO EARTH

There's nothing more irritating than talking about your close encounter to a disbeliever. So forget about the authorities. As soon as you stop shaking, call the most gullible member of your family.

# A WORD ABOUT TIPPING

Never tip an alien until you are returned safely to earth. Then give him 15% of what you think your life is worth.

## SHOULD AN ABDUCTEE WRITE A THANK-YOU NOTE?

When an abducted human has been returned to Earth safe and sound, going back to the site of the abduction and leaving a thank-you note or even a few words on a visiting card ("Inblyk, it was divine!") takes very little time.

## WHEN AN ABDUCTEE IS NOT RETURNED TO EARTH

Keep in mind that hollering uses up oxygen. So when you finally arrive at your abductors' destination, don't fly off the handle if you find out your luggage went to the wrong planet.

If you wind up having to spend the rest of your life on Mercury, you should try to be philosophical about it.

Actually, when you consider it, it's really not so terrible. After all, Mercury might be uninhabitable, but it's still not as bad as Detroit.

# ABDUCTION ETIQUETTE FOR EXTRATERRESTRIALS

*Whether he has abducted an Earth inhabitant for a quick little UFO joyride or a one-way trip into the void, an alien should always use the occasion to show he can be a good host. No self-respecting alien would want to read in an Earth paper that the human was found wandering along a highway the next day, unable to speak because he'd never been so insulted in all his life.*

## UFO ETIQUETTE

*It is bad manners for an alien craft to intentionally scare a commercial airline pilot. But it sure is fun.*

## USING THE GOOD SILVER

*If you're treating your Earth abductees to an "authentic alien banquet"—complete with five-course meal and extraterrestrial folk songs—you will naturally want to use "the company droids"—the sterling silver.*

*However, if you're just picking up a bucket of chicken, the plastic droids will do.*

# EARTHLINGS LIKE SOUVENIRS

*Try not to blame an abductee if, when you land back on Earth, you catch him trying to walk off the Mother Ship with an ashtray in his pocket. Earthlings are genetically incapable of going someplace without bringing back souvenirs, and you can't expect one to pass up the chance to take an abduction keepsake.*

*Actually, it's your own fault. Don't you know an abductee would gladly pay for a metal paperweight in the shape of your ship? Or an Official Abduction Flyswatter? Or a backscratcher with four spindly fingers?*

*So if you're going to continue abducting, and you don't want to keep losing guest towels, jettison that hydroponic forest on Level 3. Open a gift shop.*

# IF THIS IS TUESDAY,
# IT MUST BE ANTARES

*But what if it's not your intention to drop your guests back off on Earth? To ready abductees for life on the other side of the universe, the considerate abductor always provides an in-flight orientation.*

*It doesn't have to be any kind of elaborate, show-biz production. Just a 15-minute slideshow with a name like "The Outer Space Experience"—something to introduce abductees to what there is to see and do, so they'll know which moons they want to go back to when they're on their own.*

*Of course, if the abductor is planning on leaving his guests on a barren planet, it would also be thoughtful of him if he were to hand out sheets containing information on supply-drop dates, predicted eclipses, edible rocks, and so on.*

# GLOSSARY

- *A close encounter of the first kind:* Sighting a UFO.

- *A close encounter of the second kind:* Finding physical evidence of a UFO.

- *A close encounter of the third kind:* Making direct contact with an alien.

- *A close encounter of the fourth kind:* Having an alien over for "coffee and."

- *A close encounter of the fifth kind:* Helping an alien pick out carpeting.

- *A close encounter of the sixth kind:* Pinching an alien on the behind.

- *A close encounter of the seventh kind:* Lending an alien a few bucks.

- *A close encounter of the eighth kind:* Slapping your hands on an alien's cheeks and exclaiming, "Oy, what a face!"

## ABOUT THE AUTHOR

SCOTT FIVELSON receives hundreds of inquiries via radio telescope asking his advice on etiquette. When he is not answering these messages, he is writing humor for *Playboy, Chicago,* and the *Los Angeles Times.*

## ABOUT THE ILLUSTRATOR

JOHN CALDWELL is a freelance cartoonist whose cartoons have appeared in numerous magazines, including *The National Lampoon, Esquire, Omni,* and *Penthouse.* He is also the author and illustrator of three books: *Running a Muck* (Writers' Digest), *Excuses, Excuses* (Thomas Y. Crowell), and *The Book of Ultimates* (McGraw-Hill). He lives in upstate New York with his wife and daughter.